WHOLE PARISH CATECHESIS

The Good News

The hundreds and thousands of inspired words in the Old and New testaments can be summarised, somewhat presumptuously, in a single sentence.

I love you and I want to be with you

These words were whispered by God in every page of the Old Testament and shouted aloud in the person of Jesus Christ. Jesus brought the Good News, confirmation that God loved us so much that he wanted to come amongst us. God's Word was made flesh. The Good News was also that God was here to stay. 'I will be with you always' (Mt 28).

The experience of the Early Church was an experience of Jesus in its midst, living with them, loving them. When the Good News was recorded thirty years and more after the death of Jesus, the resulting gospels were more than accounts of the life and teaching of Jesus. Each word was alive with the presence of the Risen Lord. Reading the Word together, sharing the Good News, was another way for those early Christians to be with Christ.

As a church we have become disconnected from the experience of a life pulsating with the presence of a living God. We have been offered a rich banquet by a prodigal God who adores us. Somewhere along the way we seemed to have settled for a diet of descriptions.

What is the Good News?
Christ is still here.
With us.
Loving us.

Breige O'Hare

Whole Parish Catechesis: Advent and Lent

FAITH DEVELOPMENT FOR THE FAINT HEARTED

*A Down and Connor
Family Ministry Initiative*

the columba press

First published in 2005 by
the columba press
55A Spruce Avenue, Stillorgan Industrial Park,
Blackrock, Co Dublin

Cover by Bill Bolger
Origination by The Columba Press
Printed in Ireland by
ColourBooks Ltd, Dublin

ISBN 1-85607-491-9

Acknowledgements:
Thanks to Fr Sean Emerson of Holy Family Parish and to the parish team and parish
groups who cooperated so willingly with this project; to the team of volunteers who
planned and co-ordinated the activitiy in the parish (Orla Camplisson, Fiona
Edwards, Mark Mc Taggart, Orla Mc Carthy, Mary Quigley, Lara and Emily Fraser,
Lou Rodgers, Margaret Gunn, Declan Brown, Sarah Loonam, Aoife Duffy, Caroline
Mc Veigh, Dolores O'Connor, Siobhan McQuaid); to Anita Ryan and to Fr Michael
Mc Ginnity for their support and advice; to Clare Gilmore, for her admin support
throughout this project; to Paul, my husband, for his patience and his proof-reading.
The material on Eucharist on pages 68 and 69 is the work of Fr Michael McGinnity.

Contents

APPENDICES

Introduction

'In summary, in order for the good news of the kingdom to penetrate all the various layers of the human family, it is crucial that every Christian play an active part in the coming of the Kingdom ... All of this naturally requires adults to play a primary role. Hence it is not only legitimate, but also necessary to acknowledge that a fully Christian community can only exist when a systematic catechesis of all its members takes place, and when an effective and well-developed catechesis of adults is regarded as the central task in the catechetical enterprise.'

International Council for Catechesis, *Adult Catechesis in the Christian Community* (U S Catholic Conference, 1992) #25.

Between March 2003 and Christmas 2003, the Down and Connor Family Ministry Office, working in conjunction with Holy Family Parish, Belfast, piloted a strategy for 'whole parish catechesis' which harnessed the collective energy of individuals and groups in the parish. The focus was the Sunday celebration in Advent. The aim was to provide suggestions for activity, discussion and prayer that would support catechesis in the homes during the time of preparation for Christmas. It was also anticipated that the resulting process could also be used at Lent to produce gospel-centred resources for use in a family context. The wider aim of the initiative was to evaluate the potential of whole parish catechesis to enable, as quoted above, 'the good news of the kingdom to penetrate all the various layers of the human family'.

This work is presented in two sections.

Section One
The first section outlines the pilot as it was planned, implemented and evaluated in Holy Family. It charts the What? Why? and How? of the project.
• WHAT is catechesis?
• WHAT is Whole Parish Catechesis?
• WHY use Whole Parish Catechesis as a model for catechesis?
• HOW did we develop and adapt the model for use in Holy Family Parish?

Section Two
The second section gives details of letters, meeting outlines, a retreat day – everything a parish might need to begin to develop the process as part of the parish Advent or Lent preparation.

I realise that there is a need for 'off-the-peg' resources that might be used with minimum effort in parish. This pilot led to the development of such a resource for use during Advent in other parishes in the Down and Connor Diocese. However, there are advantages to using a process which involves parishioners of all kinds from the beginning. It draws on the talents of many gifted parishioners and involves people who would not think of themselves as having a contribution to make. Valuable opportunities are created for groups who tend to work in isolation in the parish to work together and to get to know each other. The process builds parish.

The process presented is not perfect and may need modification for use in your parish. Many of the suggestions, for example, the Retreat day (pages 65-71) can also be used separately as part of parish formation and training.

Holy Family Parish Pilot Project

What is Catechesis?

This may seem to be a very basic question. However, given that the Oxford English Dictionary defines catechesis, quite narrowly, as 'teaching a series of questions and answers', it might be a helpful starting point to clarify the Catholic Church's much broader understanding and use of the word.

The early Church used the word 'catechesis' to describe the process which instruction in the faith was to assume: learning to imitate the faith and lifestyle of the believing community. Those being catechised were to live the teaching of the catechist in word and deed.

Over the centuries, and, notably, as a result of the Council of Trent (1545-63), faith was identified with belief in stated doctrines. The associated catechesis focused on summarising those beliefs and ensuring that they were taught as clearly as possible, usually to children and primarily in the form of question and answer catechisms.

Vatican II has heralded a significant shift in thinking which is reflected in subsequent church documents. There is a new and sustained emphasis on our call to '… union with Christ, who is the light of the world, from whom we go forth, and towards whom our whole life is directed.' (*Catechesi Tradendae: Catechesis in our Time,* John Paul II 1979 #5). The union mentioned here is not some sublime, esoteric state but an accessible, intimate relationship with the person of Jesus Christ. The call to union is a call to have faith not in some*thing* (doctrine) but in some*one* (Jesus).

If the role of catechesis is to help us to imitate the faith, it must serve to help us to grow in intimate relationship with Christ. Deepening intimacy requires more than the exercise of the intellect elicited by the question and answer catechisms. It involves an engagement of the entire being – body, mind, heart, soul. The purpose of catechesis is thus to enable us to be increasingly open and responsive to the Lord's loving embrace in a way that allows the Lord to permeate and transform every aspect of our being.

Catechesis needs, therefore, to embrace all aspects of life experience – family life, formal education, work, social action, recreation – in order to provide contexts for growth in intimate relationship with Jesus Christ.

Furthermore, catechesis is not a solo activity; it requires the formation of an individual in the context of a deep and intimate association with a faith community. It is not enough to say that a parish has a catechetical process; every parish community needs to recognise that it is called to be a catechetical process.

What is Whole Parish Catechesis?

'Whole Parish Catechesis' is a paradigm for catechesis which is currently gaining support in the United States. Centred on the Sunday liturgy, its aim is to unite the formal instruction provided by the parish (homilies, schools, children's liturgy, sacramental preparation, parish programmes) with the informal sharing and living of faith in everyday family and parish life. The ultimate aim is always to create a community wherein the faith is shared through lived experience. Bill Huebsch suggests a simple formula for implementing a strategy for whole parish catechesis (*Whole Community Catechesis in Plain English,* p 32).

- During Sunday Mass, the homilist leads everyone, including himself, to ask a single well-focused, real-life question, prompted by the scriptural text of the day.

- The purpose of the question is to draw the believer more deeply into the gospel and to explore a personal response e.g. Beatitudes – which one stood out for you? How will you allow it to affect your life?

- During the following week the question of the week is used throughout the parish for faith-sharing at the beginning of each gathering, e.g. when the choir gathers to rehearse; when volunteers meet on Monday morning to count the collection; in classrooms and at assemblies in school; when families are driving home, having supper or finding a few moments to talk

Huebsch's experience of this process is encouraging:
> … the most amazing thing begins to happen. Solidarity begins emerging as everyone in the parish shares the same gospel story all week. It begins to feel as though the gospel, once the business only of the homilist, is now everyone's business. People naturally begin to see the hand of God in their lives. And most importantly, individually and communally, folks echo the faith in their own lives and hear the echo of it in the lives of their mates.

Catechesis happens in this process because parishioners are helping each other to recognise the gentle presence of a God who is intimately connected with every breath of existence, every glorious and mundane detail of daily life. They assist each other in attending to an experience of God: an experience, however subtle or elusive, which will draw them into a deeper relationship with God and with each other.

Why use Whole Parish Catechesis as a Model?

The traditional approach to catechesis has been to bring people out of their homes to attend programmes. The weakness of this approach is that it tends to encourage separation between *taught* catechesis and *lived* catechesis, the latter referring to catechesis experienced in the ordinary events of family life.

 It is an unhelpful separation; the family is the first faith community within which we experience and respond to the call to intimate relationship with Christ. The challenge is to help families to know and love Christ, alive and active in the joys and brokenness of family life. The challenge is also to encourage families and the wider parish family to experience itself as the body of Christ – to be a catechising community – intimately associated with the living, risen Lord and possessing the power to proclaim the good news.

Whole Parish Catechesis supports home-based, family-centred catechetical discussion and activities. It provides opportunities to bring the good news to life, to bring the good news *into* life. The relevance of the good news, the presence of the living Lord and the transformative power of that presence can be attended to and experienced amidst the pots and pans of family life.

Holy Family Parish – A Snapshot

Holy Family Parish in North Belfast, is one of the largest parishes in the Diocese of Down and Connor. With over 10,000 parishioners, the parish encompasses three churches, seven schools, a youth club, a day centre, a pastoral centre and a community centre.

It has an active pastoral council, over thirty parish groups and a youth faith development group which employs two secondary and two primary school teachers for a number of hours each week to work on youth faith and relationship issues.

The parish functions as one unit but parishioners still tend to identify with their own church and its particular congregation. The areas around each of the three churches are quite different in character. One church is situated in what for many years was the domain of Protestant business people and which contains many examples of large Victorian residences. Another church, bombed before its opening in 1980, now finds itself in a mixed residential area. The third church, Holy Family Parish Church, has a congregation which still experiences the painful effects of sectarian tension, although parish and community relationship building have greatly reduced the manifestations of such tensions.

Holy Family Parish was chosen for this pilot because:

- The pilot would be responding to an expressed need: a recent parish survey highlighted parishioners' desire for help with prayer and relationship with God.

- With three church congregations of essentially different character, the results of this pilot would apply to a wide range of parish situations.

- The talent and goodwill in the parish, and the continuing openness of the parish team to encouraging greater lay involvement, would mean that the pilot had a good chance of success. In addition, even if the pilot failed, there would be a willingness to engage with the reasons why. Either way, the pilot would be a useful learning experience.

Whole Parish Catechesis in Holy Family Parish

A parish survey undertaken in 1999 highlighted Holy Family parishioners' desire for support with faith/prayer. When the Family Ministry Office approached the parish team with a proposal for piloting Whole Parish Catechesis (hereafter referred to as WPC), the strategy was viewed as one way of addressing this desire.

Holy Family Parish and the Family Ministry Office agreed to collaborate on a short-term pilot. The intention was to provide a flavour of WPC without committing huge amounts of parish and Family Ministry Office resources to a plan which might not translate well into an Irish context. Advent was chosen as an appropriate time to run the pilot because it had a particular focus and a specific time frame. It was also hoped that an Advent pilot might offer parishioners an antidote to the materialism of the pre-Christmas frenzy.

Adapting the American model for a Belfast parish
In planning the pilot, we took account of the following:

* For many Irish people, faith is a very personal, private affair and the prospect of sharing any aspect of that faith, or of personal details relating to family life, might prove threatening.

* Twenty-first century life moves at a fast pace. Finding time to talk with family members – about anything – is increasingly difficult. It is therefore unrealistic to expect any family to share explicitly about its faith if family members are not in the habit of talking about their thoughts and/or feelings to each other.

* Some parishioners might be more comfortable with action rather than discussion as a first step. Asking parishioners to undertake a small practical activity might, quite naturally, lead to discussion and perhaps faith sharing.

The initial task of this form of catechesis was therefore to find a way of prompting discussion/sharing in families/parish that:

- Proved non-threatening

- Inspired action, discussion, and reflection

- Laid the foundations of an understanding of faith based on relationship with Christ and with each other as the Body of Christ

Three associated tasks were identified, all linked by a common purpose: spending time together – building relationships.

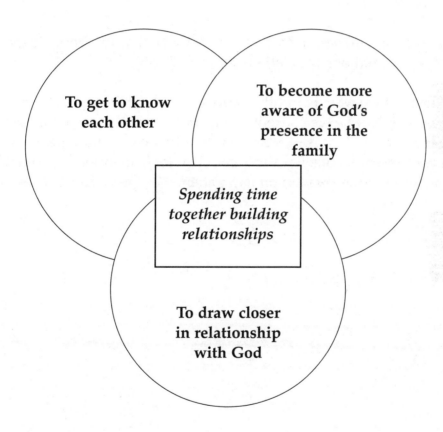

Aims of the Pilot

1. To identify one topic for parishioners to think or talk about and a related simple activity emerging from the Sunday scripture and relevant to day-to-day experience of family life.

2. To enhance, in a small way, the experience of our parish as a community of prayer and Christian action.

3. To support/assist families in their activity and prayer through Sunday liturgy, school and other parish groups.

4. To encourage chat/prayer/activity in a way that enhances family/parish relationship and, ultimately, relationship with God.

In beginning the pilot we were painfully aware that, whilst we were aiming for whole parish catechesis we were concentrating on the Mass-going population. This is not the whole parish and ways need to be found to include those people on the margins or outside of parish life. For this pilot, therefore, attention is given not to the 'lost sheep' but to the sheep who remain patiently in the paddock, sheep also in need of food.

Main Components of the Pilot

SUNDAY LITURGY
Lay person introduces theme before Mass begins. Prayer used in Advent wreath liturgy and after communion during Lent.

SUNDAY GOSPEL
Homily introduces theme for week.

PARISH GROUPS
Begin meeting by praying/talking about theme.

FAMILY
Talk about theme.
Pray about it.
Do something about it.

CHILDREN'S LITURGY
Activity/worksheet picks up on theme. Encourages parental involvement at home.

ELDERLY/ HOUSEBOUND
Asked to pray each week for and with the families of the parish.

SCHOOL
Assemblies.
Worksheet for home/school use.
Booklets for individual reflection (teenagers).

BULLETIN
Highlights theme: one thing to talk/pray about; one thing to do.

Summary of Stages of the Pilot

Stage1: Publicity and Recruitment

Month	Meeting	Involving	Purpose
March	Initial Presentation	Holy Family Parish Team	To discuss feasibility of idea
Mid September	Introduction Meeting I	Representatives from parish groups, activities and schools, interested individuals	To establish common understanding of catechesis and common sense of vision/purpose To enlist members for group To distribute resources that would assist in deciding topics
End September	Introduction Meeting II	Parish Liturgy Groups	To give basic introduction to purpose and invite participation/collaboration

Stage 2: Preparation of resources and parish groups

Month	Meeting	Involving	Purpose
October	I. Core Group Meeting	14 volunteers from introduction meeting including 4 teenagers from each secondary school	Review purpose Decide themes for Weeks I-IV
	II. Core Group Meeting	14 volunteers from introduction meeting including 4 teenagers from parish secondary school	Work on topic/ activity for weeks I & II
	III. Core Group Meeting	14 volunteers from introduction meeting including 4 teenagers from each secondary school	Work on topic/ activity for weeks III & IV
Early November	• Individual contact with parish group to communicate topics and encourage involvement (letter followed by phone call from core group members).		

• Individual contact with parish group to communicate topics and encourage involvement (letter followed by phone call from core group members).

• Workshop session with Readers and Ministers of Eucharist
– to foster deeper understanding of links between liturgy and life and underline God's presence in both,
– to encourage, especially Ministers of Eucharist, to bring topics (large print booklet) and prayer to sick and elderly.

Stage 3: Implementation

Month	Meeting	Involving	Purpose
Mid November	Practical Arrangements	I. Liturgy Group Representatives	To discuss how topics might be integrated into liturgies.
		II. Core Group	Feedback from parish groups. Finalise practical arrangements.
		III. Parish Team	To agree final arrangements.
		IV. Ministers of the Word	To finalise rota for introduction of theme at start of Masses

• Topics/Activities produced as booklet which is distributed after Masses on the Sunday before Advent.

• Members of Core Group address congregation at Masses to introduce project and invite participation.

• Project outlined in Parish Magazine.

• Worksheets to schools and Children's liturgy Group.

Month	Meeting	Involving	Purpose
End November/ December	Pilot Project implemented	Families Parish Groups	Undertake activity that is relevant to theme e.g. Third World Group had lunch during 'giving week'.
Early January	Evaluation	Parish Core Group Parish Team	

Resources Produced

The following resource materials were produced and are offered here as follows:

Pages 22-23: Booklet containing weekly themes and activities:
- Given to every family.
- Large print version available.
- Each theme presented individually on front of Weekly bulletin.
- Used by secondary schools in class/assembly and for individual reflection by pupils.
- Used by parish groups as basis of prayer and reflection.

Pages 24-27: Homily Notes
- Samples included for Weeks one and two.

Page 28: Ideas from Parish Liturgy Committees.

In section two: Introduction to Catechesis (see Initial Meeting, pages 45-55) and A Parish Retreat Session (pages 65-71).

ADVENT: HOW ARE YOU GETTING READY THIS WEEK?

Week 1: Signs

In the gospel we hear of the second coming of Jesus. Jesus is already present in our midst, in the ordinary events of our day, in the kindness and generosity of people we know or meet. Recognising the Jesus amongst us, acting through us in our ordinary lives, will help us to recognise Jesus when he comes again.

To do: Watch out for acts of kindness from family, friends or strangers and thank them for their kindness or do an unexpected kindness for someone else.

To think/talk about: Think of the people you know who reassure you that there is goodness in the world. Spend a few minutes with your family or friends remembering one/more of these kind people. In your prayer, either on your own or as a family/group, thank God for signs of his presence in your world in those people.

Prayer
Dear Lord,
Thank you for the people we know who have been kind to us. We thank you especially for … (name of individual/s) and we are very grateful because she/he …. Help us to recognise and to thank people for their kindness. Help us to realise that their kindness is a sign that you are living and working in our world.

ADVENT: HOW ARE YOU GETTING READY THIS WEEK?

Week II: Balance

In the gospel this week, we hear about John the Baptist in the wilderness. A wilderness can be a place of confusion but also a place of life and growth. In the run-up to Christmas, life can seem to be a bit of a wilderness. The frenzy of shopping and preparation can be enjoyable but also draining and stressful. Can we find time to do the things that give us life? How can we make sure that we set aside enough time to help us to grow closer to God and to the other members of our family?

To do: Take time this week to do something the whole family enjoys when preparing for Christmas. List the things you least like about Christmas preparation. Decide as a family to eliminate at least a couple of these things from your list.

To think/talk about: Think of how you and your family are preparing for Christmas. How much of your time is taken up with shopping, decorating and celebrating? Where is Christ this 'Christ'mas?

Prayer
Dear Lord
Keep us safe and sane as we prepare for the celebration of Christmas. Help us to find you in our celebrations.

ADVENT: HOW ARE YOU GETTING READY THIS WEEK?

Week III: Giving

In the gospel, John the Baptist tells us how we can bring Jesus into our lives. By sharing and giving example to others we can help to bring Jesus into the lives of those we meet.

To do: Perform simple acts of kindness to family, friends and strangers, at home, in school/places of work and in our neighbourhood.

To think/talk about: Think of simple ways we can help others. Remember people who have given us help throughout our lives, and how we felt about receiving it. What was it like to know that you had the support of family and friends – especially in the times you didn't want, or perhaps didn't know that you needed help?

Prayer
Dear Lord,
Thank you for all the times others have helped us. May we become aware of the needs of others and how we can help them. Remember those who find it difficult to accept the help of others or find it hard to ask for it

ADVENT: HOW ARE YOU GETTING READY THIS WEEK?

Week IV: Expectations

In the gospel this week, we hear of two women who are expecting. At this time of year we all have different expectations for the Christmas season. Social and personal expectations are some of the main causes of holiday stress. For the best of reasons, we can place huge burdens of expectations on ourselves and perhaps miss out on the joyful expectation which is a part of this season. We wait in expectation; the Christmas story is the beginning – New Birth, New Beginning.

To do: Look at everything your family does to prepare for Christmas and the expectations we have of our family members and ourselves. Agree to share out certain tasks over the next few days – so that no one person is left with everything to do.

To think/talk about Talk to your family about your expectations for Christmas. What are you most looking forward to? Is there someone who is not looking forward to the same thing as you? Why might this be?

Prayer
Dear Lord,
As we look forward to Christmas, may we feel a little of the joy that Elizabeth's baby felt in the womb when he was in the presence of Mary and the unborn Jesus.

23

Homily Notes

Week I: Signs

And then they will see the Son of Man coming in a cloud
with power and glory. *(Luke 21: 25-28; 34-36)*

*In the gospel we hear of the second coming of Jesus. Jesus is already present in our midst,
in the ordinary events of our day, in the kindness and generosity of people we know or
meet. Recognising the Jesus amongst us, acting through us in our
ordinary lives, will help us to recognise Jesus when he comes again.*

Suggestions for Homily

- Advent begins by looking into the future to the second coming of Christ. It finishes by remembering the first coming, the first Christmas.

- We find ourselves in between those two comings and needing to be strengthened so that we might wait with patience and with hope.

- We might find that strength in remembering a different kind of coming of Christ – the Christ who has come into our presence and who is with us now
     in our sacraments
     in each other.

- We so often use the word 'grace' and perhaps do not appreciate the full significance. There are many definitions but it might be helpful to think of grace as the gift of God's self to us, God's love poured into our lives.

- In the sacraments we receive God's grace, God's very self, Christ's self.

- In our presence to each other we can be in many ways sacramental; imperfect though we are, we can be channels of God's grace, channels of God's love.

- We can be evidence of God's presence, of the presence of the risen Christ in our world.

- It is very difficult to appreciate that presence in ourselves; to appreciate that even in the smallest acts of kindness, often done for very mixed reasons, we can somehow bring God's love to others.

- It is easier to see God's love at work in others and in doing so to be reminded that God – the Risen Christ - is with us and active in our worlds. Maybe that would be a good place to start – we can return in a few weeks time to yourself as a sign of God's love but we'll start by looking at others.

- This week we are going to invite you to take some time to reflect on kindness as you've seen it shown by others, little acts of love that you have noticed.

- You are invited to pay attention, as in the readings, to Christ's coming, to consider these kindnesses as evidence of that coming

---

Refer to booklet:

To do: Watch out for acts of kindness from family, friends or strangers and thank them for their kindness or do an unexpected kindness for someone else.

To think/talk about: Think of the people you know who reassure you that there is goodness in the world. Spend a few minutes with your family or friends remembering one/more of these kind people. In your prayer, either on your own or as a family/group, thank God for signs of his presence in your world in those people.

For Your Prayer
Dear Lord,
Thank you for the people we know who have been kind to us. We thank you especially for … (name of individual/s) and we are very grateful because she/he …. Help us to recognise and to thank people for their kindness. Help us to realise that their kindness is a sign that you are living and working in our world.

Homily Notes

Week II: Balance

A voice of one crying out in the wilderness, 'Prepare the way of the Lord.'*(Luke 3:1-6)*

In the gospel this week, we hear about John the Baptist in the wilderness. A wilderness can be a place of confusion but also a place of life and growth. In the run-up to Christmas, life can seem to be a bit of a wilderness. The frenzy of shopping and preparation can be enjoyable but also draining and stressful. Can we find time to do the things that give us life? How can we make sure that we set aside enough time to help us to grow closer to God and to the other members of our family?

Suggestions for Homily

- Perhaps too easy to dismiss our hustle and bustle in preparing for Christmas as distraction – in it there is evidence of:
  - Desire to do the best for our families.
  - Desire for enjoyment in the midst of the darkness and dreariness of winter.
  - Desire for a full life.

- In so many ways God wants these things for us too – God wants us to experience life to the full, to have deep joy – even in the midst of life's darkness and difficulties. God wants our families to have the best that life has to offer.

- God's 'best' – in gospel terms today this is described as 'the salvation of God' but this can seem a very distant and cold term. Think of it instead as God's dream for us – a dream which is so much more than we could ever ask or imagine.

- If we focus entirely on one aspect of the preparation for Christmas we risk overlooking the bigger dream – God's dream.

- To stay in touch with the bigger dream we need to find a balance between the things we have to do in the midst of this Christmas rush and the things that we enjoy, activities that help us to live life as a family and live it fully. We need to spend time with God, even a few minutes each day.

- It is difficult to find that balance and to use time in a way that will help us to get to know each other and God. The pressures that are put on us by society are very real and we can feel failures if we do not go along with the flow.

- The invitation is to spend more time with family/friends who know and love you – no matter what you can do or not do.

- The invitation is also to spend more time with God – the God who understands why you want or feel the need to do so much at Christmas but who longs to spend time with you as you are now, not as you think you should be. A God who wanted to be so close that he came to earth to be with you. A God who can use any time we might snatch with him to remind us of the love and the dreams he has – even in the midst of our struggles – our 'rough ways' our own wilderness (Gospel).

- How to find that balance: small ways.

Suggestions in the booklet
To do: Take time this week to do something the whole family enjoys when preparing for Christmas. List the things you least like about Christmas preparation. Decide as a family to eliminate at least a couple of these things from your list.

To talk/ think about: Think of how you and your family are preparing for Christmas. How much of your time is taken up with shopping, decorating and celebrating? Where is Christ this 'Christ'mas?

For Your Prayer
Dear Lord
Keep us safe and sane as we prepare for the celebration of Christmas. Help us to find you in our celebrations.

Ideas from Parish Liturgy Committees

Suggestions to link Advent Wreath with Parish Advent themes

The themes, prayers and 'to dos' for each week could be made available in a booklet form to use with the Advent wreaths on sale in the parish. During the Sunday liturgy it is suggested that the congregation are provided with the opportunity to say the prayer for the week when the candle is being lit.

It might also help if the prayer was displayed in a prominent place – perhaps in church porch and/or behind the Advent wreath, so that people visiting the church during the week might be reminded of it.

To give this prayer a context for everyone it was also suggested that a reader introduce the theme for the week in advance of the procession.

A reader might be appointed, if possible, to the same Mass over the four weeks. This reader would be additional to the people on the usual Sunday reading rota. S/he takes responsibility for ensuring that the celebrant has a written copy of the structure for this short piece at the beginning of Mass.

The suggested structure is as follows:

1.   Before the procession comes from the sacristy, the appointed reader, from the lectern, says two or three sentences (written down) to introduce the theme for that Sunday.

2.   Procession with priests and reader(s) from the usual rota.

3.   The appointed reader lights the candle on the Advent wreath and the priest says the prayer for that week (See booklet).

The coordinators from each section of the parish are willing to take responsibility for finding readers willing to introduce the theme and light the candle. If any more readers are required, they can be found in the core group established to develop the Advent themes.

Summary of Evaluation of the Pilot

The evaluation was conducted in three ways. At Sunday Mass, the parishioners were asked to complete a short questionnaire (see pages 34-35). These were returned to boxes at the back of each of the three parish churches or to the parish office. This questionnaire was distributed to members of parish groups. Oral feedback was elicited by members of the core group, parish team etc. Secondly, an evaluation process was undertaken with the parish team. Finally, the core team reviewed its experience of the planning process and implementation. A summary of the feedback from those three sources is given below together with a brief evaluation of the pilot with respect to the original aims (page 16).

1. Parishioners

Comments were received orally and in writing from approximately 100 parishioners. With the exception of one parishioner who thought the initiative was too idealistic and formal, the pilot project met with a very positive response. Parishioners felt the material was well presented and the suggestions down-to-earth and helpful in preparing for Christmas. Some of the comments about the ways in which it made a difference to family preparation for Christmas are quoted below. They are taken from the written evaluations and are representative of the general themes expressed by parishioners.

> 'It made me and my family think about others instead of just ourselves. It also made us think that we didn't really need to go with all the fuss.'

> 'I like the list of things to do. My family were able to share lots of the good and not so good things to do.'

> 'Helped to focus, even in a small way, on the presence of Christ in Christmas.'

> 'Made us more conscious of links between praying, thinking and doing.'

2. The Parish Team

Feedback from the parish team was positive.

- They valued the fact that all parishioners were invited to participate. They particularly liked the suggestion that the elderly were the parish's 'contemplative communities' and acknowledged as having an important role to play by praying with the other parishioners at this time.

- Contacting and inviting representatives from each organisation to the initial information meeting was an effective way to invite involvement.

- With three churches in the parish, it was very helpful to have the parish united each week around a single theme.

- Booklet and handouts (for school/children's liturgy) were very accessible.

- An encouraging number of parishioners had mentioned having a greater awareness of praying throughout Advent.

- Homily notes for the first two weeks in Advent gave a detailed insight into ideas underpinning themes chosen. (A shortened format – bullet points – was used for the second two weeks. The more detailed format was preferred.)

Further suggestions emerged from team members:

- It might be helpful to choose themes that were very distinct. Some of the existing themes seemed to overlap in areas.

- Higher quality presentation of booklet (glossy *vs* photocopy).

- Use of laminated paper for prayers – for parishioners to keep.

- Giving parishioners candles to use with prayer (common practice in this parish).

- Undertaking evaluation at end of Advent, rather than after Christmas – to increase response rate to written evaluation

3. Core Group

The Core Group at the centre of organising the pilot reviewed the initiative by reflecting on feedback from others and on the experience of core group members. Again, the general sense was positive and they were reassured by the responses they received from other parishioners. Group members commented particularly on how the project brought the various groups of the parish together for a common purpose.

All those involved in preparing and presenting the material said that it had encouraged a more prayerful preparation for Christmas in their own homes. It had also given them a feeling of having contributed to something worthwhile. The teenagers especially were pleased to be able to work as equals in this group.

Some suggestions for future modifications emerged:

- Rather than spreading preparation meetings over three months, bring groups together in mid September and follow this with 4 consecutive weekly meetings in October. Provide outlines for school assemblies.

- Take into account also that some schools have a full exam timetable for most of December and that Advent may not be the best time for this initiative.

- Collect more feedback from individuals/parish groups in relation to their planned activities around the weekly themes. Greater communication with parishioners about this related activity.

- Increase involvement in the initiative by:

  - Personal invitation.

  - Visiting/contacting individuals from groups who have not responded to the initial invitation.

  - Greater emphasis on role of Ministers of Eucharist/neighbours in getting elderly/sick involved in praying.

  - Advertise the themes in 'non-church' places:

  - Posters (with cartoons) in shop windows or hairdressers.

  - Booklets in local parent/health/leisure centres.

  - Short feature in local community newspapers.

Were the Aims of the Pilot Achieved?

As with all matters of faith, it is impossible to measure precisely the degree to which all or any aims are achieved. However this does not imply absolution from the responsibility of appraising the effect of the pilot strategy in the parish. What follows is a brief evaluation of the pilot with specific reference to the original aims – indicated on page 16.

AIM 1: To identify one topic for parishioners to think or talk about and a related simple activity, emerging from the Sunday scripture and relevant to day-to-day experience of family life.

It is evident that the pilot achieved this purpose. By drawing on the experience of parishioners of differing ages and from a wide variety of backgrounds, the core group successfully identified topics and developed activities that were very accessible to individuals, families and groups in the parish.

AIM 2: To enhance, in a small way, the experience of our parish as a community of prayer and Christian action.

The process enhanced the experience of a community of Christian action in various ways. The parish works hard to celebrate the activities of the many groups active within it and this was another valuable occasion for mutual affirmation. However, as in all parishes, faces of people generously contributing to parish life can be very familiar but there is often neither the time nor the opportunity for such people to chat together and to get to know each other. The meetings associated with the planning and implementation of the pilot afforded parish group members and other interested individuals the opportunity to exchange names, to chat about the work of their particular group and to work collaboratively for a common purpose.

The experience of a community of prayer and action was also evident as the core group laboured to connect scripture with daily life in a way that would be relevant for other families. We joked over tea and cream buns. We swopped insights about the gospel passages, listened as suggestions for activities were bounced about the small groups and we discovered new meaning in these familiar texts. The experience of community on those evenings was tangible. We shared faith.

The extent to which the experience of Christian community was translated at the level of the wider parish community is unclear. However, the pilot did make a positive contribution to the existing communications and community network in the parish. The three churches of the parish were united under common themes. Oral feedback indicated that the suggestions were accessible and the relevance of the activities and prayers meant that parishioners and their families could connect with what unfolded over Advent.

The pilot could have been enhanced by greater communication of the associated activities of the various parish organisations and schools. Other methods might be explored to encourage children to involve parents more in school-based activities. The core group suggestions for contacting and involving more people (see page 31) might serve to enhance the community dimension.

AIM 3: To support/assist families in their activity and prayer through Sunday liturgy, school and other parish groups.

The initiative involved as many groups as possible in discussing and acting on the material. Consequently, families were exposed to the topics through the Sunday liturgy, their primary and secondary school children, the scouts, the children's liturgy and, possibly, through the parish group to which they belonged. The extent to which children brought home the material discussed in school and the extent to which parish groups engaged with the process varied. Some parish groups, for example the *Lectio Divina* group, used the material as the basis for their Advent prayer; others, for example the Developing World group, connected their usual Advent activities with the themes.

Parishioners also indicated that the initiative was a recognition of their need for help with prayer. Vocal, community prayer was encouraged and supported by the prayers used at Mass, school assemblies, etc. Families and individuals did use the booklet form of the themes as a focus for private prayer and reflection.

Prayer is a huge and complex area of pastoral concern. The four short weeks of Advent could hope to make a tiny contribution to addressing the needs identified by the parishioners themselves in the parish survey. However, by encouraging a blend of activity and prayer, by introducing prayer which is relevant to the family preparation for Christmas as well as to the liturgical preparation, it is evident that this form of catechesis can help support and assist families in their activity and prayer.

AIM 4: To encourage chat/prayer/activity in a way that enhances family/parish relationship and, ultimately, relationship with God.

From the oral and written feedback it is clear that this pilot helped some families spend time together working and talking about the Advent themes. Even if this time was only a few minutes a week, it afforded opportunities for shared experiences, experiences which enhanced relationships with each other.

Any parish activity can at best hope to provide help with a single step on the life-long journey towards relationship with God. Families are our first place of experience of Christian Community and perhaps our first significant encounter with God. We learn about relationship with God, we learn about God's love, we can receive God's love in the context of family life. Although impossible to measure, the contributions made by the pilot to family relationships and the explicit connections made between family activity and God alive and active in our midst contributed in a small but significant way to some parishioners' experience of God/Christ.

Preparing for Christmas Together

How are you getting ready this week?

Signs – Balance – Giving – Expectation

The aim of this initiative was to put the parish at the service of families of all shapes and sizes as they prepared for Christmas.

A diverse group of parishioners met to decide on something simple to think/talk about, something to do and a simple prayer, all around a single gospel-based theme for each week of Advent. All of the parish – groups, schools, children's liturgy, families, clergy, religious, elderly and housebound – were encouraged to participate.

We need to know if this was helpful to you in your own family circumstances. For this reason, I would be grateful if you could complete and return this short questionnaire.

4. Did this initiative help you, your family or parish group prepare for Christmas?

If YES
In what way did it make a difference?

If NO
What might have helped?

34

1. Where did you come across the 'Preparing for Christmas' material? (Tick ALL that apply)

a. Got copy of 'Preparing For Christmas' booklet ☐

b. Read it on the front of the weekly bulletin ☐

c. My children covered the topics
   in the children's liturgy ☐

d. I have primary school children and they were
   talking about it in school/at home. ☐

e. I have secondary school children and they were
   talking about it in school/at home ☐

f. A minister of the Eucharist brought it to me
   or my relative/friend ☐

g. In my parish group (Name? _____)

2. Please circle the appropriate answer

1 = poor   3 = satisfactory   5 = Very good

a. Booklet/bulletin presentation   1 2 3 4 5

b. Ideas for activities   1 2 3 4 5

c. Ideas to think about   1 2 3 4 5

d. Prayer suggestions   1 2 3 4 5

e. Homilies on the Advent themes   1 2 3 4 5

3. Which of the following was possible for you? (Tick all that apply)

a. Thinking about the weekly themes
by myself ☐   with family ☐   with parish group ☐

b. Using the prayer
by myself ☐   with family ☐   with parish group ☐

c. Doing suggested activity
by myself ☐   with family ☐   with parish group ☐

Conclusion

Above I have outlined the church's emerging understanding of catechesis, an understanding which has growth in intimacy with Christ as its ultimate goal. As with all close relationships, such intimacy requires that we meet Christ regularly and frequently. The fact that Christ is present in every atom and aspect of our lives means that, in theory at least, such meetings should not prove difficult. However, our previous emphases on knowing about Christ rather than knowing Christ, have dulled our collective powers of recognition of Christ's presence in our midst. We need help in making connections, in remembering, celebrating and living in the presence of God's Word embodied in the Risen Christ, 'I love you and I want to be with you.' We need help, quite literally, to bring the gospel to life, our life.

The measure of the success of any catechetical approach will, therefore, be the extent to which it contributes to our knowing and walking with Christ in our daily lives. This initiative had the ubiquitous communication glitches and last-minute frenzies that add 'colour' to parish life. However, amid the successes and struggles, it provided an effective glimpse of the potential of whole parish catechesis as a means of reaching into the homes of parishioners and heightening awareness of Christ's presence in their midst.

The initiative was a small step.

It slowed down some of the people for some of the time – an achievement in itself in the busy weeks before Christmas. It encouraged parishioners to be more attentive and aware of the simple events of their own lives – an important early step in heightening their awareness of God in the midst of those events.

It provided accessible suggestions for families: small opportunities to chat and work with each other in ways that built relationships. It made a small contribution to nurturing relationships within families in a way that eventually will contribute to an understanding and experience of relationship with a loving God.

It enhanced, for many, the experience of Holy Family Parish as a community of prayer and Christian action. It provided lay people with further opportunities to support each other: families produced prayer/activity resources for use in other families. This was one of the greatest strengths of the initiative. The resources were simple and accessible and, for this reason, they were used.

The extract from 'Adult Catechesis in the Christian Community' included in the introduction presents us with a truly wonderful vision of a catechising community. There are many ways of achieving this community and this is appropriate; we are gloriously various, created to embody the glory of God in so many different ways. This strategy, based on whole parish catechesis and developed for the Irish context, is one means available to parishes to enable 'the good news of the kingdom … to penetrate all the various layers of the human family …'

The Good News
'I am with you always'
Mt 28

Christ is still here.
With Us.
Loving Us.

A Process for your Parish

This section contains everything you might need to try this project in your own parish. It begins with letters of invitation which can be used to gather the group. Also provided is information to send in advance of your initial meeting; this ensures that those attending have a basic understanding of the purpose of the project and the expected commitment.

For your convenience, pages 40-44 are available from Down and Connor Family Ministry website (thefamilyministry.net). They can be down-loaded and tailored to suit your own needs.

Information to distribute in advance of the initial meeting

Letter of Invitation to Parish Group Representatives

Dear ...,

Enclosed is an outline of a pilot project we hope to undertake in the parish in Advent (Lent) 200_. We are keen to make this project simple and relevant and would value your help in doing so.

There will be an information meeting on *(time, date)* at *(address)*. The purpose of this meeting is to:

- Discuss the purpose of the project and present a suggested structure.
- Encourage early and active participation of parishioners/parish groups.
- Enlist members of a core group (12-16 people) to develop the initiative in the parish. Information on the proposed commitment of core group members is also enclosed with this letter.

It would be very much appreciated your and/or another representative from your group could attend this meeting. However, if this is not possible we would be grateful for the opportunity to meet with you at a more convenient time. You can let us know if you are able to attend or if you want to arrange another time, by ringing xxx xxxx.

We look forward to seeing you.

Information to distribute in advance of the initial meeting

Letter of invitation to parents / teenagers
Given to named individuals, supported with personal contact.
The information in parentheses modifies letter for use with teenagers.

Dear ...,

Enclosed is an outline of a pilot project we hope to undertake in the parish in Advent/Lent 200_. The project aims to use all the resources of the parish to support families in their preparation for Christmas. We want to make the project as relevant to family life as possible and would value your help in doing so.

There will be an information meeting on *(time, date)* at *(address)* to present an outline of the plan and to enlist members of a 'core' group to develop the initiative in the parish. At the meeting will be parents (some teenagers) like yourself (parents/ parishioners) and representatives from parish groups. It would be great if you could join us. You might also think about joining the core group – I have enclosed details of the expected commitment of members.

Let us know if you can come.
We look forward to hearing from you.

Information to distribute in advance of the initial meeting

Whole Parish Catechesis: Sharing the Good News Together

Who helps us to grow in relationship with God and so to develop our faith?

OUR FAMILIES
Imperfect though they may be, families have the potential not only to tell us about God but to show us God's love in action. They are the first place we learn about God and the first chance we have of experiencing Christian community.

OUR SCHOOLS
Here we learn the details of our faith. We are prepared for sacraments and in our schools find another experience of Christian community.

OUR LITURGIES
Liturgies have the potential to provide us with opportunities to celebrate our faith together, to receive sacraments as part of the parish family.

GROUPS IN OUR PARISH
In our parish groups we have further evidence of our faith in action. In meeting together to pray, to play, to serve others, we reach out to the parish family. We have the potential to bring God's love fully alive in the group to which we belong and for the group of people we serve

These people are all doing great work. Can you imagine what it might be like if we could harness the energy of all the individual activities in the parish and focus on central, simple themes emerging from the Sunday gospel? What would it be like to have families, schools and parish groups discussing, praying and acting upon these themes in a united way and, in doing so, perhaps building relationships with each other and with God?

The idea of getting the whole parish family involved in thinking about and acting on the Sunday liturgy has already been tried with great success in the US. In (parish name) we hope to run a pilot – in Advent/Lent 200_ – to gauge its potential for ourselves. A very basic outline of the pilot is given overleaf.

A look at what's involved each week

SUNDAY LITURGY
Lay person introduces theme
before Mass begins. Prayer
used in Advent wreath liturgy
and after communion during
Lent.

SUNDAY GOSPEL
Homily introduces theme for
week.

PARISH GROUPS
Begin meeting by
praying/talking about theme.

FAMILY
Talk about theme.
Pray about it.
Do something about it.

CHILDREN'S LITURGY
Activity/worksheet picks up
on theme. Encourages parental
involvement at home.

**ELDERLY/
HOUSEBOUND**
Asked to pray each week for
and with the families of the
parish.

SCHOOL
Assemblies.
Worksheet for home/school
use.
Booklets for individual reflec-
tion (teenagers).

BULLETIN
Highlights theme: one thing to
talk/pray about; one thing to
do.

What time commitment will it require of you?

At the introductory meeting you will be asked to consider volunteering for the core group which will help develop this initiative in the parish. It may be useful for you to know the commitment that this will require.

Early September	Introductory Meeting	Why Are We doing this?
Last Week September	Meeting I 7.30-9.30pm	• Why are we doing this? • Resources we might use • Review themes for Weeks I-II • Work on Week I
First Week October	Meeting II	• Review of Week I • Themes III-IV • 3 small groups – each take one of remaining weeks
Second Week October	Meeting III	• Final review of materials • Discuss distribution and communication in parish
	• Materials printed/copied • Liaise with Parish Organisations	
Second Week November	Meeting IV	• Feedback on plans of Parish Organisations • Organising liturgy/materials • Allocating tasks
Beginning January	Evaluation Meeting	

The Initial Meeting

Suggestions for Content of Initial Information Meeting

Aims

- To discuss the purpose of catechesis and present an outline of the proposed structure for Advent/Lent

- To encourage the early and active participation of as many parish groups as possible

- To enlist members for the core group which will identify themes and develop the initiative in the parish

Outline

- Opening Prayer and Introduction

- Icebreaker

- Overview of Evening

- What is Catechesis?

- Where does it happen?

- Sharing in Groups – over a cup of tea

- How might it be encouraged?

- What we might do as a parish during Advent/Lent

- Recruiting volunteers

1. Introductions and Opening Prayer

Introduce self/other facilitators. Promise an outline of the meeting in a few minutes but first an appropriate reflection from Oscar Romero followed by a chance to get to know each other a little.

> This is what we are about.
> We plant the seeds that one day will grow.
> We water seeds already planted,
> Knowing that they hold future promise.
> We lay foundations that will need further development.
> We provide yeast that produces effects far beyond our capabilities.
>
> We cannot do everything, and there is a sense of liberation in realizing that.
> This enables us to do something and to do it very well.
> It may be incomplete, but it is a beginning,
> A step along the way,
> An opportunity for the Lord's grace to enter and to do the rest.
>
> We may never see the end results
> But that is the difference
> Between the master builder and the worker.
> We are workers and not master builders,
> Ministers and not messiahs.
> We are prophets of a future not our own.
>
> *Oscar Romero*

2. Icebreaker

Suggestion: Photocopy cartoons with a faith/church connection on to individual A4 pages. Cut each cartoon into 3-4 pieces and distribute at random among the group (for a larger group use different colours of A4 sheets to make it easier). Group members are asked to find the rest of their particular cartoon. This gets them into groups of 3-4 where they talk about:

- Why am I here?

- What am I hoping will happen?

Gather a few of the expectations when you bring whole group together again.

3. Overview of the Evening (On flip chart/Overhead)

> - What is Catechesis?
>
> - Where does it happen?
>
> - How might it be encouraged
>
> - What we might do as a parish during Advent/Lent?

4. What is Catechesis?

Take suggestions from group members about the words that come to mind that they associate with 'catechesis'.

Accept the suggestions without judgement. In an Irish context suggestions will possibly centre around doctrines and liturgical practice.

Some of their suggestions will be represented in the overhead (below). All these are important tools in catechesis and can be affirmed as such. However they are tools: their purpose is to bring us to greater knowledge of and love for the person of Jesus Christ.

The facilitator might wish to take one or two thoughts about or initial reactions to what has just been presented.

What is Catechesis? Suggested overhead:

> Catechesis aims
>
> 'to put people not only in
>
> touch, but also in
>
> communion and intimacy
>
> with Jesus Christ'
>
> *General Directory on Catechesis #80*

5. Where/when does Catechesis happen?

Read two stories to illustrate.

I. The Gospel from First Sunday of Advent

> Year A: 'You do not know the day when your master is coming … the son of Man is coming at an hour you do not expect.' *(Mt 24)*
>
> Year B: '…you do not know when the master of the house is coming…if he comes unexpectedly, he must not find you asleep.' *(Mk 13)*
>
> Year C:'…there will be signs…then they will see the son of Man coming …'*(Lk 21)*

II. The monastery

> There is a story told about a monastery where the monks had become demoralised about their vocation and were constantly bickering with each other. The abbot was at a loss to know what to do in the midst of so much tension and despair. He went to his provincial who told him that the trouble would pass. He was certain of this, he said, because he knew a secret that he had chosen to keep to himself until now. He knew that Jesus had returned to live amongst us and had chosen the monastery as his home. One of the monks – and he was not sure which one – was Jesus. Although Jesus at this stage did not want his identity revealed, surely he would not let tension tear the community apart.
>
> The abbot returned home, amazed at the news that Jesus had chosen their community. One by one, he proceeded to inform the monks of the special guest in their midst. Not knowing which of their companions it was and anxious to show love and concern to Jesus, the monks began to treat each other with a new respect. Confident that Jesus was with them, they reached out with vigour and enthusiasm into the neighbouring towns and villages and soon the monastery was filled with novices, eager to live in the midst of what had become a thriving, loving community.
>
> The abbot went with great joy to tell the provincial of the transformation of his community. He wanted to know if the provincial might reveal the identity of the monk who was Jesus. The provincial replied, 'You want to know because you think that the presence of this monk has transformed your monastery. There is no monk. Jesus has always been in your midst. The transformation has happened because you were helped to recognise this.'

What message might these stories have this evening?

Perhaps they suggest that, rather than simply seeing the coming of the Son of Man as a future event, we are asked to combine the message of these two stories and to heighten our expectation of the coming of Christ whilst being attentive to Christ's presence amongst us.

> Amongst us
>> in our liturgy
>> in the Word
>> in the Eucharist
>> when we gather to pray or talk about him

There is more to be said about where Christ is present in our midst. A little scarier is the realisation that Christ is uniquely present within each one of us and that in our words and actions – no matter how ordinary the situation – we have the potential to make the Christ who is present within us evident to the world outside us.
(Provide an example from your own life of someone behaving towards you/others in a way that reminds you of Christ's presence.)

Ask people to go back into their small groups to discuss experiences of being Christ for someone or of being reminded of the Christ in someone.

If this sharing happens over a cup of tea and buns/cake (forget the dry biscuits that seem to be a mandatory part of church gatherings!) then it might prove relaxing for the groups – especially those members who are not used to talking in small groups in this way.

Take feedback from the groups. Emphasise that what is happening in the room is catechesis:

- We are recognising Christ within.
- We are sharing stories about Christ.
- We are gathered in his name.
- We are, in a small way, getting to know Christ better through his action in our lives.

We don't know each other very well and some people might understandably be uncomfortable talking about their deepest thoughts. That's ok but could you imagine what it would be like if we could invite and support family members, or encourage members of parish groups who have maybe known each other for years, to sit and talk about Jesus:

- How his teaching impacts on them and relates to the ups and downs of their own lives.

- How Jesus is working in and through them to touch others.

If this were happening, even on a small scale, we could see how important our homes are as places where Christ lives. Our entire parish – every aspect of parish life – becomes a place where parishioners and visitors to the parish might come to know and to love Jesus.

This may sound very idealistic but it is good to remember that this ideal was the everyday experience of life in the Early Church. They had their wrangles and disputes, their trials and joys; in all of this was an awareness of Christ present in their midst working in and through each member of the community.

We may not share that experience at present, but Christ is still with us.

An exercise:
Look around the room and notice everything that is blue. Pay close attention. All the blue items.

Now, without looking again, name me something in this room that is yellow. It's hard isn't it? In a way we have become less accustomed to looking for the yellow – the risen Christ in our midst. However, when our eyes become attuned, we will realise that the world is peppered with yellow: filled with the presence of the risen Lord.

We are only going to take baby steps in this process. In the opening reflection we are watering existing seeds, perhaps sowing new seeds too.

Ask if there are any questions so far (apart from: How are we going to do this?)

6. How might it be encouraged?

To encourage an awareness of Christ present and a deepening of relationship with Christ, we need to remember a few things first.

Most people don't think of their houses as places where God is present.
(You might use the cartoon overleaf as an overhead to introduce this point)

They tend to associate God and faith with church, or with the school which prepares their children for sacraments. It's an attitude which the church had actively encouraged to ensure a consistent approach to teaching doctrines and dogmas.

However in recent years the realisation is that teaching about God is no substitute for facilitating an *experience* of God. Such experience is vital if we are to help each other grow in relationship with God. With this in mind we need to consider:

Bear in mind

- Talks and liturgies are not enough! Jesus is out there in parish homes and groups. We need to help each other to see and to relate to him there.

 - There is a greater chance that we will encourage each other to talk about Jesus/God if we are finding ways to spend time together and talking about other things.

- Faith sharing is not easy. An activity that is in harmony with the gospel might provide the basis for less threatening conversation.

He's not in here, mister
Try next door.

7. What can we do in this parish?

- Refer to background information included with letter of invitation.

- Mention briefly the different ways we have available to us to grow in relationship with God. *(Included in handout on page 42)*

- Underline the good work that all these people and groups are already doing in the parish

- Pick up on the idea already mentioned in that handout that it might be a very energising experience if we were to support each other by bringing the various strands of parish life together, and by focusing on common activities and common themes emerging from the Sunday gospel.

- Suggest that Advent (Lent) is ideal because it has strong themes and definite time boundaries. It is focused and manageable.

- Mention that the role of the core group, that emerges from this evening's meeting, will be to:
  - look at the Sunday gospels,
  - decide themes,
  - decide ways of communicating those themes to groups/ individuals.

- Reassure those present that scholarly knowledge of scripture is not required – background resources will be provided. They have more than enough experience and skill to make this project simple and effective.

- Suggest to them that they have already been working with the first gospel this evening, and with a possible theme eg 'I am with you', as they chatted over a cup of tea about people who were heaven-sent in their lives. The buzz in the room was obvious, people were comfortable. They were talking about something simple, yet relevant and, as we soon discovered, very affirming and uplifting. What we did here tonight is a sample of what we might hope to do in the parish – in homes, schools and in parish groups.

- Refer to handout opposite, also included with information sent in advance of meeting. This shows the possible target groups and gives an initial indication of how it might play out in the parish.

SUNDAY LITURGY
Lay person introduces theme
before Mass begins. Prayer
used in Advent wreath liturgy
and after communion during
Lent.

SUNDAY GOSPEL
Homily introduces theme for
week.

PARISH GROUPS
Begin meeting by
praying/talking about theme.

FAMILY
Talk about theme.
Pray about it.
Do something about it.

CHILDREN'S LITURGY
Activity/worksheet picks up
on theme. Encourages parental
involvement at home.

ELDERLY/
HOUSEBOUND
Asked to pray each week for
and with the families of the
parish.

BULLETIN
Highlights theme: one thing to
talk/pray about; one thing to
do.

SCHOOL
Assemblies.
Worksheet for home/school
use.
Booklets for individual reflec-
tion (teenagers).

8. Recruiting Volunteers

Reinforce the Central Purpose–

> 'to put people not only in
> touch, but also in
> communion and intimacy
> with Jesus Christ'

in touch with – through our everyday conversations and actions we can bring God's love to life in us and through us.

in communion and intimacy – as we help each other to recognise God/Christ in the everyday. In the tangible expression of God's love, in God's support and comfort as experienced through others, we come to a greater awareness of who God is. As we share our faith – in words or in actions – we believe that 'Where two or three are gathered in my name, there am I in their midst.'

We hope we can make the resources of the parish available to help parish families/individuals to act, think and talk in a way that will contribute to a greater appreciation of the liturgical season, the deepening of family relationships and growth in relationship with God.

Big targets – life-time targets, not Advent/Lent targets but we can do something, as mentioned in the opening reflection from Oscar Romero, by watering the existing seeds and planting new seeds and perhaps never seeing the fruits. Small seeds, watered by faith.

What next?
What we target them with is very much up to us. For this reason I'm asking for volunteers to work on themes for Advent/Lent based on the Sunday gospel.

(Note to organiser: you might want to have handpicked some of the group to ensure a good balance of talent and contacts etc. See Suggested Composition of Core Group, page 79).

To conclude the meeting
- Remind group of the time commitment (refer to handout, page 44):

- Invite questions or thoughts about what was covered this evening. It is a lot to take in so you can invite people to approach you after the meeting, give them a contact telephone number etc.

- Thank those who came for information but who cannot offer time in this way. Promise future contact in mid October to keep them informed and to discuss how the good work of their group/family might dovetail with the parish preparation for Christmas.

- Encourage contact to give feedback about this evening's session, to volunteer ideas to find out more about what's going on.

- Ask for their prayers for the group who will be working on the themes.

- Ask the group members who are interested to stay behind to arrange the date of the next meeting. Give them materials to prompt reflection for the next meeting.

- Close the session with the Lord's Prayer, praying that what happens in our homes, in our parish and in this project, be according to God's will, God's dream for us.

Materials given to prompt thinking

Relevant extracts from:
- *Living Liturgy*, Joyce Ann Zimmerman, CPPS., Thomas A. Greisen, Kathleen Harmon, SND de N., Thomas L. Leclerc, MS. (Liturgical Press: Collegeville, Minnesota, 2000, 2003, 2004).

- *The Complete Children's Liturgy Book: Liturgies of the Word for Years A,B,C*, Katie Thompson, Illustrated by Jennifer Carter (Kevin Mayhew 1996).

- *Footprints in Faith:Take-Home Leaflets for Every Sunday of the Catholic Lectionary for Ages 7-12*, Katie Thompson (Twenty-third Publications, 1999).

Advent/Lent Core Group Meeting I

(1½-2 hours duration)

Aims

- To decide themes for Advent/Lent Weeks I and II.

- To provide whole group with opportunity to work on Week I activity and prayer in order that we might reach a shared understanding of the necessary content and style of material.

- To distribute material for Weeks III & IV in advance of next meeting.

1. Opening Prayer

2. Introductions	Who we are and why we each have chosen to get involved (might want to share this information in pairs first – less intimidating before individuals introduce themselves to larger group).
3. Review material distributed (at Introductory Meeting). Suggest topics for Weeks I & II. Emphasise keeping ideas and language simple.	Small groups. Collect ideas in large group (use flip chart). Agree themes.
4. Tea	As for Introductory Meeting – have decent food here.
5. Decide details for Week I: • A few introductory sentences linking theme with gospel. • One thing for families to think/ pray about. • One thing to do. • A simple prayer.	This can happen over tea. Small groups discuss options. One person feeds back to large group. Whole group decides content for Week I – not looking for consensus but most favoured and practical option.
6. Materials for Weeks III & IV distributed. Whole group asked to consider possible themes for discussion at next meeting.	Split core group into 3 smaller groups, each of which will take responsibility for deciding details for a week of Advent/Lent.

7. Closing Prayer

Group leaders collate material from 5 above to use
as the basis of small group work at next meeting.

Guidelines for Developing Questions and Activities

The Holy Family booklet (pages 22-23) in Section One will give you some examples of questions and activities. Below is an outline of a process to help you to develop you own.

- Read the gospel for the Sunday.

- Read the supporting materials from *Living Liturgy* (or other liturgical material) and the children's liturgy guides
  - What words stand out for you as you read and listen?
  - What themes are present? e.g. caring, forgiveness, healing, judgement, courage, confusion?
  - What phrase(s) – especially everyday phrases come to mind as you listen?
  - e.g. He was a 'God-send' 'No time like the present' 'Chill Out'

A flip chart or a big piece of paper on the floor or wall is good for jotting down ideas so that everyone can see them.

- Agree on a theme to get you started – it can be modified as you work with it. Using this theme, create a question that might help people
  - To get to know Jesus by thinking about or praying with this gospel.
  Or/
  - To Identify God's presence and action in their lives.
  Or/
  - To recognise what the passage means for them in their own circumstances – to see themselves as God's Word made flesh

- The question needs to ask for a personal response – The aim is not to prompt a discussion about 'the faith' but to encourage groups and families to talk about what is important to them, especially their relationship with God/Jesus.

- The question should be in plain English with a version suitable for children.

- It needs to be a question that cannot be answered with a yes/no.

A few examples

First Sunday of Advent (Cycle C)
Gospel Luke 21: Watch for Christ's coming

- Where have I seen Christ this week?

- Who has been 'an angel', a God-send', for me in the past week?

  Children's version:
- Who has shown God's love to me this week?

First Sunday of Lent (Cycle C)
Gospel Luke 4: Temptation in the wilderness

- What do I have – possessions, job, good name – that help me to feel secure?

- Relying on God in tough times means …

   Children's version
- How does God / Jesus help me when I am sad or frightened?

Suggesting activities

Deciding on a theme and creating a simple question should help clarify possible activities.

Suggest activities which might involve the family working together on a simple task, e.g. writing thank-you cards to people who have been helpful over the past week, identifying a charity needing donations and working together to gather money, clothes, furniture etc.

The activity needs to challenge the family to live out the message of the week's gospel, e.g. Advent week one – actively looking for signs of God in our lives; Lent week one – looking at the possessions we use to give us a false sense of security – what can we give up this week so that others might live better quality lives?

Discussion/ Sharing Guide for St Bognet's Parish: How your material might be used

This is a suggested outline for the prayer of families or groups in your parish. It is a suggestion – you will know what will work in your parish.
Underline for them that participation is encouraged but is voluntary. The outline is adapted from an outline provided in *Handbook for Success in Whole Parish Catechesis*, Bill Huebsch, Twenty-Third Publications, 2004. p 79.

This can take place at the beginning of the normal meeting for the group, even if the group does not have a usual time slot allocated to prayer in this way – e.g. finance group, choir.

Families could use this version after dinner and even though it might feel a bit awkward at first, they could find a comfortable way to make it their own. If the themes chosen are practical and down-to-earth there is a greater chance of family members being interested in discussing/ sharing around the themes.

Coming to Prayer

Leader
We'll stop for a moment in the midst of all our activity to prepare for some time with God and with each other.

A few seconds of quiet.

Listening to God's Word

Leader	The Lord be with you
All	And also with you
Leader	A reading from the Holy Gospel according to …
All	Glory to you, O Lord

Read all or part of the gospel reading.

Leader	This is the gospel of the Lord
All	Praise and glory to you, Lord Jesus

Sharing

Leader: This week in the parish we are thinking about this question:
Question/thought for reflection
Maybe we could say a little about what has been in our minds or in our hearts as we consider the question.

Each person speaks for an agreed time, without interruption. If the member goes beyond the time, the leader needs to intervene. It is sometimes better if each sharing is honoured – a few seconds pause between contributions can serve this purpose – but not discussed by other members. It can degenerate into a discussion session and it can discourage the shyer members from making further contributions if they think their contributions are going to be 'worked with'.

Closing Prayer
You might want to close the sharing by praying in one of the following ways:

Our Father – said aloud.

Spontaneous prayers.

A short moment of silent prayer – introduced as such and concluded by saying the 'Glory be'.

Listening to a recording of a hymn or other kind of sacred music.

Advent/Lent Core Group Meeting II

(1-2 hours duration)

Aims

- To review material collated from last week and so ensure common understanding of focus and content

- To agree themes for Weeks III & IV (Lent III-VI).

- To produce materials on these themes for weeks II-IV (Lent II-VI).

1. Opening Prayer

2. Review last week's material by revisiting group's understanding of purpose of this initiative and check if material (language, content etc) suits purpose.   See sample from Holy Family Parish, pages 22-23.

3. Agree themes for Weeks III & IV (Lent III-VI).   Discuss in large group (go into small groups if ideas prove to be too disparate).

4. Using last week's material as a guide, produce materials for weeks II-IV (Lent II-VI).   3 (Lent = 5) small groups (as agreed last week, each taking a single week). Leader appointed to act as spokesperson and give feedback.

5. TEA

6. Continue work of 4 above.

7. Groups ensure agreed ideas put on paper.

8. General feedback from each group.

9. Closing Prayer

Core Group leaders take material from each small group and collate text – as for Week I.

Advent/Lent Core Group Meeting III

(1-2 hours duration)

Aims

- To review material produced to date.

- To discuss further communication with parish/parish groups.

- To agree and produce additional resources.

1. Opening Prayer

2. Brief review of material produced to date.	Core group leaders distribute collated text.
3. What additional material do we need?	Possible options: • Text produced in booklet. • Large print version. • Tape cassette version. • Children's Liturgy Sheets. • School class/assembly material. • Bulletin inserts. • Homily notes/liturgy outline.
4. Jobs allocated from 3. Some work might require help from outside group or communication with others, eg if parish has liturgy committee.	• Small groups work on producing above material. • Agree date with group leaders for completion.

5. Spreading the word
Discuss necessary communication with parish – this will vary from parish to parish. You might wish to refer to pages 63-75 below which provide suggestions as to how parish groups and parishioners might be informed and encouraged to participate.

Pages 63-4   Follow-up meeting with representatives from parish groups, schools, etc., to discuss themes, materials, etc., and to elicit feedback about how they see themselves becoming involved (invitation letter and evening outline).

Pages 65-71   Short retreat session – afternoon/evening for parish ministries, parish groups or individual parishioners.

Follow-up Meeting

Draft letter to Parish Group Representatives

Dear ...,

As promised at the end of the information evening, we would like to keep you up to date with the Advent/Lent Initiative in the parish. We would appreciate it if your group/school/organisation could join with us in implementing the initiative. This should not require you to do more than the good work you already undertake in the parish. Our purpose is simply to explore with you the ways your group might link with the proposed Advent/Lent themes and activities.

For this reason we are holding a short (1 hour) meeting for parish group representatives and would welcome your attendance – or the attendance of a representative from your group (school, etc)

Time:

Date:

Venue:

Could your confirm your availability to attend this meeting by ringing xxx xxxx?

I look forward to seeing you.

Outline of Evening

7.30pm   Opening Prayer and reintroductions

The proposals for Advent/Lent

Your response to what you have just heard –
What will work? What might need adapted?

How would you see your group/school/organisation getting involved?

What do you need to have, or to happen in order to really feel a part of this initiative?

8.30pm   Closing Prayer
Tea (Optional)

Note to Organiser: Parishes often have groups of very good people working in complete isolation. This is a chance for a bit of 'bonding'. Use every opportunity to get people talking to each other: icebreaker at the reintroductions, small groups to discuss initial response to plans with feedback to larger groups, tea at end.

A Parish Retreat Session

Linking Liturgy and Life

The aim of the session is to help participants towards a renewed appreciation of Christ present in the Eucharist, the Word and in the everyday events of life.

- Introductions
- Icebreaker
- Overview of the Session
- Christ Present in the Word
- Christ Present in the Eucharist
- Feedback
- Prayer with the Word: 1 Thessalonians
- Break
- Word made Flesh in US
- Closing Liturgy – The table of the Eucharist and the Family Table

1. Introduction – Facilitators

2. Icebreaker
'Celebrations' different variety of sweets – Find 2-3 people with same kind of sweets
(a)   Introduce self
(b)   Say a little about why you are here. (Or why you want to be a minister of Word/Eucharist.)

3. Introduction to Session Aim

I am with you always...' (Mt 28:20b)
Link participants' desires – their reason for being there today – with God's desires. During this session the aim is to spend some time reflecting on the God whose desire beckons us here today and on deepening our awareness of God's presence in all aspects of our lives.

(When we say God we also mean the Risen Christ, so for the purposes of this session the two terms might be interchanged.)

We are going to paying attention to Risen Christ present
- in the Word
- in the Eucharist
- in the people and events of our lives.
Therefore the aim of our session is to deepen our awareness of the experience of Christ present in liturgy and in our lives.

4. *Christ Present in the Word: Text of talk*

I want to begin by looking at the Word as we know it in the New Testament and how that was regarded in the early Christian community.

First I want to remind you, very briefly, of how the gospels came into being. From the birth of Jesus to the writing of the last gospel was approximately a century. The biblical scholar, Raymond Brown divides this century into thirds with each third representing a stage in the development of our sacred New Testament texts:

> *The first stage* – the life, ministry, death, and resurrection of Jesus.
> *The second stage* – the early disciples, often eyewitnesses, preached and proclaimed Jesus. They learned about Jesus in the process. The letters (Epistles) were written in this period.
> *The third stage* – very simply, four people ('The Evangelists'), living in different places, took the Jesus tradition – everything they experienced and learned and understood about Jesus in the second stage – and put it into what we know as the four gospels.

It is important to understand what was communicated in the texts that were written down and to do so requires us to go back and get a glimpse of the early Christian community in the second stage – again this is much simplified but you are getting a simple but accurate picture of the essence of that early community.

Jesus had died and risen. The eyewitnesses to Jesus' life were present in the midst of the community. Not only were the stories about Jesus' life and teaching alive but the community recognised the Risen Christ alive in their midst.

They had a tangible sense of the presence of the Risen Jesus with them. It didn't stop the bickering and the in-fighting because they were only humans, but they knew that Jesus was there and – as we will pick up a little later – they were convinced that Jesus was going to return in their lifetime.

What was fixed in the sacred texts of this community then was not just words but the presence of Jesus. The texts were an extension of the experience of community, a community which had within it the Risen Christ. The texts in their turn fed the community and deepened their awareness of the presence of the Risen Lord. Both were inextricably linked. Christ/God was present in a way they could not fully understand – Paul talks about 'seeing through a glass dimly' in Corinthians – but they did not doubt that presence.

To understand something of the sense of Christ's presence in the Word, I am going to use an image of that presence that is part of our own reality – the breath. It's an image that is used in relation to God in the Old Testament so, like many of the words we use in relation to God, it has a meaning we can understand but it also carries something of the mystery of God that is beyond our understanding. Imagine yourself reading the Word and that your breath represents the presence of

God, the presence of the Risen Christ. Not only are you saying the words of the text as you read but you are also experiencing the movement of your breath from you, through the words and out into the community. The breath is life-giving. Without it you would not exist.

Your breath is added to the air, to the breath that is already present in the community; it contributes to what they breathe in. It becomes part of who they are and they take away part of that breath. They go home with part of their physical being changed in a minuscule undetectable way by the breath that they have all shared.

Like all analogies, it is not enough to capture the mystery of what is happening when you proclaim the Word but do you get a sense of Christ's life-giving presence going through you, through your words to be shared by the community, to be absorbed into the individuals, to change them in an undetectable way?

We are talking about the Word and saying words and then carrying more, meaning more than just the words. I want to stop for a moment and consider what God is trying to say to us through the Word. Again I am simplifying the message but to some extent God's 'bottom line' is simple and our entire Old and New Testament is a reflection of God's desire to communicate with us by trying as many different ways and words as possible. God's simple message is: I love you and I want to be with you.

It is whispered in the pages of the Old Testament and shouted, proclaimed in the person of Jesus Christ. I love you and I want to be with you – so much that I will come to earth, I will make myself vulnerable and weak, and I will become one of you to show you how much I love you, to show you how much I want to be with you.

So the presence of the Risen Christ in our sacred texts is also the constant presence of God's love and God's infinite desire for us. Jesus Christ is God's last word – all that needs to be said about the depth of God's love and longing for us (Hebrews). In opening the texts, in proclaiming the Word, we are immersed in the presence of the Risen Christ and bathed in God's love and desire. It is in our every breath, shared in community, taken into our lives and with the potential to make every word and action an opportunity for the sharing, for the channelling of God's love.

How many of us are aware of the power of what we open before people on a Sunday, or is it that, in the words of one parishioner who spoke to me about the practice of his faith, 'We are conditioned not to expect too much'? How can we be more aware? How can we be more open to the presence of Christ in the Word?

Facilitator can help here by affirming what the participants are doing in their prayer and reflection on the gospel.
Feedback: small groups/person beside – What stands out for you in what has been said?

5. Christ Present in the Eucharist: Text of talk

The Eucharist is at the heart of the church's whole life because at the heart of the Eucharist is the real presence of the crucified and risen Lord. He is present as God and man, soul and divinity.

Scriptural Witness
In the Eucharist we see Jesus as the one who brings about a unique bond of love between God and us by pouring out his own life's blood in sacrifice.
Mt: 'This is my blood of the covenant'
Lk: 'This cup is the new covenant in my blood which will be poured out for you'.

Jesus tells us to eat and drink, i.e. to ratify the new covenant he asks us to eat some sacrificial food – Jesus himself given up for us and given back to us. What Jesus has done is he has taken the Passover meal, the celebration of the rescue from slavery in Egypt, and transformed it. In the Eucharist Jesus is saying to us, 'I want to be with you; I want to live in you; I want to make my home with you; I want you to be free from slavery and sin and to have life to the full. Jesus is the new Moses, rescuing us from the power of death and offering us a new life.

So it is not a static, motionless Jesus who is present to us in Eucharist. It is the self-giving and self-sacrificing Jesus who longs to be with us. It is this Jesus who comes to meet us in Eucharist and who welcomes us. We are at one with him – one body – one flesh with him – in the one sacrifice – we are united with Jesus in his offering of himself to the Father.

Historical Perspective
From middle 2nd century on, St Justin, St Cyril, St Thomas Aquinas, Martin Luther were writing and reflecting on the real presence of Jesus at the consecration of Mass. Debates, discussions about nature of that presence followed. What actually happens to the bread and wine?

By 800AD Eucharistic theology and devotion were less about active participation by the people but more centred on the 'real presence' and how it came about. There was a lot less emphasis on the meaning and purpose of Eucharist in the life of the Christian community – Jesus' command to 'take and eat' was beginning to mean in practice 'come and gaze'.
- Fewer people receiving communion – (our great grandparents were receiving communion once a year.)
- Another effect of this emphasis was to see the Eucharistic presence of Jesus only in terms of the consecration at Mass. That is what mattered in the celebration of Eucharist. Christ's presence in the Word of God, the priest, the people were ignored.

Whereas now, with renewal of liturgy in Vatican II, we are growing in awareness of Jesus present in community of baptised believers, present in the Word of God proclaimed. In the Document on the Liturgy of Vatican II, 'It is Jesus himself who speaks when holy scriptures are read in church.' (Recall Road to Emmaus story – Jesus read the scriptures for the disciples – pointed out the texts that were about himself.) Jesus is present in the priest who represents him as Good Shepherd gathering his people.

This new awareness has changed everything – new emphasis on active participation: from the very beginning of celebration, the Liturgy of the Word and the Eucharist are one single act of worship.

God's Word is spoken As it is spoken, God becomes present to us. God speaks to us about his desires for us – hopes and dreams – plans and dreams for us. God's invitation to us in the Liturgy of the Word is to be open – not just to a message or a bit of good advice – but to God himself.

God wants to open our eyes to see who we are. We are daughters and sons in whom God delights, with whom God wants a deeper relationship.

God in his Word wants us to see the 'big picture' – the big plan he has for us. It's so easy for us to get caught up in our worries and struggles – concerns – so that we end up with a narrow vision of life. God is saying look 'your life story finds its meaning in the amazing and wonderful plans and dreams I have for you now as well as in the future. The life you live now is part of my plan. Life may be boring and dull but your love and goodness makes a difference to the world – is part of my life and my plan to heal and save the world.' The Word of God lifts our eyes towards new horizons.

We are all near-sighted and hard-of-hearing so we need Christ to open our ears and eyes, to touch our hearts, to inspire us. So in the Word of God Christ invites us to be open. If we allow the Word to touch our hearts we will slowly but surely become more open – more ready to receive Christ, more ready to invite Jesus in the Eucharist. When the Word of God is received it calls forth from us an invitation to Jesus to come and stay with us, live in us, share our life. The Word of God opens us up for deeper relationship with God/Christ. We can look at the Word of God as offering us good advice, information, guidance and support. That's fine – we can take what we need and go away. And yet, first and foremost The Word of God invites us to be open to being touched – meet my God in the depths of our hearts, moved to want a relationship with God. That's what listening at the table of The Word is all about. When we come to the table of the Eucharist itself we issue our invitation to the Lord – come and stay with us. Live in us. Christ's response to our openness is to make his home in us. He keeps the promise he made in John's Gospel: 'Jesus said: if anyone loves me he will keep my word and my father will love him, and we shall come to him and make our home with him.' (Jn 14:23)

6. Feedback – small groups

7. Prayer with God's Word: Outline of points to cover

Propose that the group tries a way of praying with the text – that they are probably familiar with – that will help them to open to God's presence in God's word.

Reinforce what was said about the Eucharist – that it is an invitation God makes to us but that it needs a response, a mutual invitation from us to God to enter into our hearts and souls as we pray with the text.
Return to the Word. Emphasise the personal dimension of Christ speaking through the Word. (Using translation of the earliest text – Thessalonians – to read in first person. Provide copies if appropriate, original text on one side, personalised text on the other.)

Prayer with 1 Thessalonians: Suggested form of words
This is a time for personal prayer. You will not be asked to share this with anyone. This isn't a prayer group session. The time is yours. It is also God's time.

I will read the text you have been given – Second Reading from 1st Sunday of Advent/Lent.

> May the Lord be generous in increasing your love and make you love one another and the whole human race as we love you. And may he so confirm your hearts in holiness that you may be blameless in the sight of our God and Father when our Lord Jesus Christ comes with all his saints. Finally brothers, we urge you and appeal to you in the Lord Jesus to make more and more progress in the life that you have been called to live: the life that God wants, as you learnt from us, and as you are already living it. You have not forgotten the instructions we gave you on the authority of the Lord Jesus Christ.
> (1 Thessalonians 3:12-4:2)

Some background: this is the earliest written text in the New Testament. This is as close as we can get to the life and times of Jesus which up until Paul started to write was recalled, remembered and talked about among the disciples. Here we have Paul writing to his first converts to Christianity and he's trying to encourage them to deepen their commitment to Christ.

Quietening exercise: (put on the music)
Find a relaxed position to sit in. Become aware of your breathing. Don't alter it in any way, just notice if it is deep or shallow. Breathe in and become aware that each breath is a gift, a gift that provides me with the air I need to live a little longer. Once you have taken a breath hold it for a few seconds and then let it out. If you are aware of any distractions or busy thoughts in your head, invite them to leave as you breathe out. As you breathe in ask the Holy spirit, God's breath, to be with you and to open your heart to God's presence.

Hear the text again but this time hear it as a letter addressed to you (personalised text below). See the other version of the text on your handout:

I want to increase my love in you and make you love one another and the whole human race as much as I love you. I want to strengthen your hearts in holiness so that you may be blameless in my sight when I return to be with you. I long for you to grow into the kind of life you are meant to live the kind of life I want for you, the kind of life I showed you. Continue to try to live as best you can and remember all that I taught you about living in my love.

Finish the prayer with Glory be to the Father …

Break

8. Need to make connection between liturgy and life, 'word becoming flesh' in us.

'Make you love one another.'

Picking up a phrase from Thessalonians: look for evidence of God's presence in your own lives – in acts of kindness or love.

Feedback
Reinforce the connection between God present in the liturgy and in your own life.

9. Closing Liturgy: Two tables – One representing altar, one the family table. Two people dressing each table in turn, saying these words:

Altar Cloth

A symbol of God's hospitality and God's desire to gather us as one family, just as we are.

Table Cloth

Gathering around the family table just as we are. God with us
  – as we are
  – whether we realise it or not
  – in the midst of our joys and struggles.

The Word

Stories that tell us what God is doing amongst his people. Stories that remind us of who we are and who we are called to be – signs of God's love in the world.

Photograph Album

Our own story in pictures.
A reminder of
  Life lived
  Love shared
  God's life. God's love in us.

Bread and Wine

Bread and wine: symbols of God's covenant:
God's love made flesh in the person of Christ;
God's love made evident in the sacrifice we celebrate;
God's desire to make a home in us.

Bread   Cup   Plate

Symbols of shared hospitality.
Our invitation to others to feel at home with us. Aware of it or not,
we bring God's love to others.

Individual Contact with Parish Group Representatives

This letter will precede contact from a member of the core group. The purpose of that contact is to determine what the parish group might do or is doing to link with the chosen themes for each week – or to suggest ways in which the parish group might get involved. Information on the various activities of the groups can be collated and communicated to the parish, e.g. in the parish bulletin, in the homily, on parish bulletin boards, etc.

Dear ...,

I enclose an advance copy of the material we hope to distribute to parishioners in late November. We would welcome the involvement of your group and would like to discuss how the existing good work of your group might be united with the proposed themes during Advent/Lent.

For this reason, someone from the Advent (Lent) Core Group will be contacting you soon for a chat about possibilities.

Yours sincerely

Letting the Parishioners know during Sunday liturgy

Outline of 2-minute Talk to give advance notice to parishioners during Sunday Liturgy – the week before Advent/Lent

With your bulletin this week you will be getting a small booklet called 'Preparing for Christmas together.' There is some information about the booklet in this week's bulletin but I would like to take a minute to tell you more about it and how we hope to use it in the parish. The booklet has been developed by a group of parishioners of different ages and from a variety of backgrounds – working with the many individuals and groups who are already doing such good work in this parish.

The booklet presents you with a theme each week of Advent (Lent), based on the Sunday gospel. For each week there will be suggestions for something to do, something to think or talk about at home, and a prayer to use if you want to. The parish will be placing itself at your service – in as many ways as possible, it will help you to stay with the theme and to pray with the theme.
(Examples of how your parish is incorporating the theme into its weekly activity.)

(The Advent wreath will be lit each week using the prayer suggested in the booklet.) The celebrant will pick up the theme in his homily. The theme will be followed in the children's liturgy and in our schools. Some of the parish groups meeting over Advent are picking up the themes as they undertake the usual pre-Christmas activity. We hope that some groups will also be able to take a little time during their meetings to talk and to perhaps pray in the way suggested in the booklet. We are also going to ask the sick and the housebound – our own little contemplative communities – to pray for us and with us using the prayer each week.

A single theme. Something to do. Something to think about or talk about with your family or friends. A prayer to use if you want.

As it says in the bulletin, we are keeping it simple. Activities are practical and easy to do. You might want to stick the page for the week on the fridge door and glance at it when you are getting the milk. The use of the booklet is on a voluntary basis. However, imagine what we might do together over Advent – families, schools, parish groups, clergy, religious – talking or praying and acting upon themes together.

It is an ideal. But it is as good an ideal as the 'tinsel and snow Christmas' we get bombarded with each year in the shops and on TV. Why don't we give it a try – even in a small way. We might be surprised with the results.

Suggested Bulletin Insert (Easily modified for use in Lent)

Getting ready for Christmas together

We work very hard to make Christmas a happy time for our families. Yet this can mean getting caught in an exhausting flurry of activity. Why not join us in trying to find some time in our busy lives to keep in touch with the meaning of the first Christmas?

It's simple. Every Sunday at Mass, a theme will be introduced for the following week. The themes have been produced by parishioners of all ages and backgrounds. A booklet detailing these will be distributed with your bulletin this week. There will be suggestions for something to do, something to talk about and a prayer to use, if you want to.

Keep it simple. The activities are practical and easy to do. The themes are very relevant at this time of the year so you don't need to organise a family conference to table a discussion – drop the theme casually into conversation or stick the prayer on your fridge door so that it catches your attention.

Why don't you give it a try?
You might be surprised with the results!

Sample of an article used in The Holy Family Parish Magazine

Help!
Results of the Parish Survey highlighted parishioners' desire for support with prayer. In continuing to respond to this need, the parish has volunteered for an innovative Advent programme of prayer and reflection being piloted for the first time in Ireland by the Down and Connor Family Ministry Office.

The aim of the programme is to encourage the entire parish community to concentrate on a simple theme emerging from the gospel each Sunday in Advent. For each theme there will be a suggested topic to think and/or pray about and something practical to do. The theme will be highlighted in the Sunday homily; the topic and the 'thing to do' will be published each week in the bulletin, together with a short prayer which people are invited to use as they wish. It is hoped that the themes will be picked up in schools and that parish groups will create opportunities in their meetings to chat or pray about the topic of the week. The sick and housebound – our own home-based contemplative communities – can join us by providing much-needed prayer support each week.

For many people, prayer together as a family will not be realistic. However, the suggestion for the practical activity might provide a prayerful way of preparing for Christmas and prompt some conversation.

The pilot programme has been developed for use in this parish by a group of parishioners who have been working in conjunction with the many parishioners and parish organisations who make an enormous contribution to parish life. Three teenagers, Sarah Loonam, Aoife Duffy and Caroline McVeigh, write of their experience of this group:

> We initially became involved in the Advent project because our experiences of prayer and community in Lourdes and Taizé helped us to appreciate how important it is to pray as a community. We wanted to give something back to the Parish, so when we heard about this opportunity, we felt it was for us.

> The first evening was an information evening and representatives from many Parish groups were present. There was a whole mixture of ages and interests present. There was time for us to talk as a group after we had been given an outline of the proposal for the project. It was good to be asked for our opinions and to have time to talk to other people involved in the Parish.

> A core group of around fifteen people agreed to take this project on for the next number of weeks and met a few times to discuss the gospel readings for the weeks of Advent. Our aim was to share what the readings meant to us personally and it was great to have such a mixture of ages and people involved, as the discussions were very interesting.

> We were given the task of picking out a word/phrase for each of the weeks of Advent and were then challenged to elaborate on that word to make it relevant for people to reflect on during Advent. We came up with practical suggestions and things to talk about during each of the weeks of Advent for the families and groups in the Parish. The priests will be using these themes in their sermons and people can then reflect on what they say, as well as discuss it with friends and family.

> Our aim is to encourage people to pray as groups, as a parish and as a family and also to talk about their faith and what matters to them. We had the opportunity to share our faith on our pilgrimage to Lourdes and Taizé during the summer and we feel it was worthwhile. We hope people will make use of this opportunity to grow in faith this Advent.

Advent (Lent) Core Group Meeting IV

(1-2 hours duration)

Aims

- To finalise preparations for the initiative
- To pray for the initiative and for parish families.

1. Opening prayer

2. Checklist to ensure all activities completed.

Examples:

- Material produced for distribution to families.

- Group/families given information in advance of initiative.

- Activities given to schools. Teachers informed of purpose.

- Liturgy agreed and all involved informed.

- Plans in place to inform parishioners of proposed activities of groups in relation to Advent Themes.

- Means of evaluation of initiative agreed: see sample evaluation sheet for distribution to families/schools/parish groups (Before Christmas).

3. Date agreed for evaluation meeting.

4. Short Liturgy to pray for the initiative and for parish families

Evaluation

Suggestions for gathering feedback

- Distribute evaluation questionnaires during the third week of Advent (Fifth week of Lent). *(Sample on pages 34-35)*

- Distribute questionnaires at Mass; leave box at back of church for returns or invite parishioners to return to parish office/other location.

- Give or post them to parish group leaders or individual members.

- Core group and parish groups collect oral feedback.

- Core group and parish groups personally invite individuals to complete questionnaires.

- Visit parish group meetings – as soon after Christmas(Easter) as possible.

- Get feedback from school children and teachers.

Core Group Evaluation Meeting

1. Opening Prayer

2. Revisit the aims. Focus discussion on extent to which these aims were fulfilled. Summary of evaluation feedback from parishioners/families. Schools/groups etc.

3. Review what was helpful; what might be modified with respect to
- our choice of themes
- our choice of prayers/activities
- presentation of ideas
- distribution of material
- communication with groups/individuals
- use of our own talents and resources
- the process we used to develop the initiative

4. Did working together help us to
- grow in relationship with each other?
- have a greater sense of ourselves and Christian Community?
- grow in relationship with God; have different appreciation of God's presence in our Christmas (Easter) preparations?

5. What was it like for us to be involved with this work?

APPENDIX I

Called and Gifted

Gathering the Leaders: knowing the gifts or talents this project will require.

Be realistic.
In the US where this idea is taking shape, they have trained catechists, paid liturgists and probably a full time salaried parish administrator. As we know these are not a common feature of the Irish church. If you are blessed with parishioners who are trained in catechesis or parish leadership, then use them. However, this project is still possible without them – you will require people of goodwill and a few of the gifts the Holy Spirit has scattered amongst the Christian community in your parish.

Leadership Group
The two or three people who will organise meetings, prepare work between meetings etc.

You will want people who can:

Collaborate   This is a business or pastoral ministry term. It means the ability to involve others. You want people who can work together, who don't feel that they have to do it all themselves, and who can listen to and work with the opinions of others. This gift can take a lifetime of experience to refine, but having people who at least understand that collaboration is essential is a good start.

Organise   It does not matter if his/her previous experience has been of organising school sports day or the apostolic workers' bazaar; if (s)he shows that they can get people to come on time to the right place, get him/her involved.

Network   This is also a business term but, translated into a parish scene, it simply means someone who seems to have a wide circle of friends and acquaintances – who knows who has just given birth, who is sick, who is taking over the local post office. These people exist, often among the group of your school parents. Ask the principal or hang around at parents' nights or at the school gates at home time.

Learn   The resources suggested are designed to make it easier to gather themes from the Sunday gospels. You want people who are open to learning from them but it is surprising what fresh insights can be gained from people who bring life experience rather than exegesis into conversation about the gospel.

Pray
Prayer needs to be at the very heart of this work. You need people who have a relationship with God, even if it is not in the form to which you are accustomed.

Listen, especially at parents' meetings, for individuals for whom Christian values and a relationship with God seem to be an important part of their lives. They are out there, many have even taken independent steps to explore their own faith/ spirituality.

This core team would also need access to basic publishing resources. Most parishes and parish schools have computers and the material will appeal if it is well presented. If an adult does not feel equipped with the necessary skills, there is a teenager in the parish school who could do the job for you.

The Core Group (Leadership Team plus 10-12 others)
This group can be gathered as a result of the Initial Meeting in the parish. Welcome volunteers but also have a few key players hand picked. Parishes differ in the groups present but a few ideas about those to invite personally:
• School RE coordinators
• Parish sister
• Youth club leaders
• Member of pastoral council
• Member of Liturgy team (Leader of Minister of Word/Eucharist)
• Member of Children's Liturgy Team
• Parents and teenagers from parish school(s)
• Member of parish choir
• SPRED (or other disability grouping)

Encourage involvement from Parish groups:
• St Vincent de Paul
• Legion of Mary
• Scouts
• Parish Social Committee
• Third World Group

Ensure that someone in the group has access to and can act as a voice for the elderly and the disabled.

Guidance for Group Leaders

Section II deals with the content of session and gives some guidance as to the process of deciding themes, questions., etc. However it may be helpful to give a few basic tips for those who are not accustomed to working with groups in this way.

A few helpful questions

In advance of a meeting:

- Does everyone know where and when the meeting will be held?

- Is the room booked and is it as you would like it?

- Are refreshments organised?

- Are you clear about the reason for the meeting and what needs to happen during the meeting?

- Are you clear about what needs to be said to ensure that other members understand what is expected from the group?

- Have you all the material you will need – a prayer for the beginning/end, pens, paper, photocopies, address lists etc?

- Have you prayed about the group and about your work in the group?

During the meeting

- Have you used your own way to make everyone feel comfortable, welcome and part of the group?

- Can everyone hear what is being said?

- Can you find a way of helping members to recall each others' names? Are you careful to use names when talking to individual group members?

- Have you introduced and explained what you hope you will do together this evening?

- Do people feel comfortable enough to speak? Even the most talkative parishioners can be reluctant to comment about faith matters – they feel out of their depth. Can you think of a fun activity to get things started?
  A few examples:
  1. Cut individual newspaper pages into three sections. Give a section to each member. Ask them to find the people with the other two sections. In that group of three ask them to talk about some good news they have heard this week – about their family/others.

2. Bible snap. On small cards write the name of a character from the bible or some word associated with our faith. Give each member a card and ask them to find their pair. Ask them to chat for a few minutes about what thoughts come to mind when you read the cards. Examples of pairs: Adam-Eve, Cain-Abel, Mary-Joseph, Mark-Luke, Pope-Rome, anger-lust.

- Can you stop at different times during the meeting to summarise what you have done together and to check that you are doing what you had intended to do? This is especially important at the end of the meeting when you need the group to decide what still requires attention.

- Are you making sure that every one has a chance to speak? Nowhere in the gospel does Jesus call us to be 'nice' yet we tend to sit through parish meetings dominated by certain individuals who are probably oblivious to the fact that they are a drain on the patience and the energy of other group members. We think that is not 'nice' to interrupt or to disagree.

A few tips when someone in the group appears to be 'overusing God's gift of speech', especially if it is seen to be distracting the group from its purpose.

- Agree with group members from the beginning that the group will give everyone a chance to contribute

- In the initial stages especially, remind the group about the agreement before each discussion. Mention that although you will be finding the contributions very interesting, you might need to interrupt to ensure that everybody gets this chance. Explain in advance that it is not your intention to be rude.

- Interrupt them but do it politely. For example, 'Can I stop you there? What you have said about … is very interesting. I'd like to hear what others have to say about that idea or maybe if they have different ideas.'

- If the comments are a distraction, listen and respond with respect but find a way of coming in and reinforcing the purpose of the evening. For example, 'That's interesting and maybe we could get a chance to chat about that later on. But with time pushing on perhaps we need to keep our eyes on … the purpose of the evening/discussion."

- Even if you are nervous and afraid of the discussion running away from you, don't be tempted to take rigid control of the group. It can be very uncomfortable to sit in a group with a leader who proceeds in a regimented fashion around each member of the group or who pounces on individuals by name rather than waiting until they want to contribute.

- There are volumes written about conflict in groups that would intimidate even well-seasoned members of the United Nations. Don't get too caught up in the idea of people as 'problems'. It is unlikely that anyone has come to cause you personally a problem. Clearly defining and keeping the group agreement to encourage contributions, ensuring that everyone is clear about what is expected of them and not getting caught up in the many issues that lie below the surface of parish life will help you survive this short-term project.

- If someone is not helping the group to complete its work and if you have had a chance to talk with them outside the group and their behaviour has not changed, ask them to leave. If they don't go, you will find that others will.

APPENDIX III

Additional Resources

The meeting outlines given in this book and the resources listed on page 55 – intended for distribution at the end of the initial meeting – are more than adequate to undertake the project.

However, if there are people in the parish who are interested in reading more or who want to get involved in the general area of faith development, a few references might point them in the right direction. Most of the texts provide signposts to the relevant church documents if more in-depth study is preferred.

Background Reading
Our Hearts Were burning Within Us: A Pastoral Plan for Faith Formation, (US Conference of Catholic Bishops, Washington DC., 1999) ISBN: 1-57455-299-6

The General Directory for Catechesis in Plain English: A summary and Commentary, Bill Huebsch (Twenty-Third Publications, 2001) ISBN: 1-58595-133-1

Horizons and Hopes: The Future of Religious Education, Eds: Thomas H Groome, Harold Daly Horell, (Paulist Press 2003) ISBN: 0-80914-154-X

Practical Guides
Leader's Guide to Our Hearts Were burning Within Us, (US Conference of Catholic Bishops, Washington DC, 2000) ISBN: 1-57455-342-9

Handbook for Success in Whole Community Catechesis, Bill Huebsch (Twenty-Third Publications, 2004) ISBN: 1-58595-308-3

Training Course for Leaders: A Practical Do-it-Yourself Kit for Forming People for Team Work, George Boran CSSp (The Columba Press, 2002) ISBN: 1-85607-359-9

Leadership For Life: Discovering Your Gifts For Christian Leadership, John Roberto (Centre for Ministry Development, 1997) ISBN: 1-890516-02-3

Everything about Parish Ministry: I Wish I Had Known (More Parish Ministry Resources) Kathy Hendricks (Twenty-Third Publications 2002) ISBN: 1-58595-199-4